Radical Sports
KAYAKING

Phil Revell • • • • • • • • • • • • •

Heinemann Library
Chicago, Illinois

Customer Service 888-454-2279

Designed by Celia Floyd
Originated by HBM Print Ltd, Singapore
Printed in Hong Kong by Wing King Tong

04 03 02 01 00
10 9 8 7 6 5 4 3 2 1

Library of Congress Cataloging-in-Publication Data
Revell, Phil.
    Kayaking / Phil Revell.
        p. cm. -- (Radical sports)
    Includes bibliographical references (p.) and index.
    SUMMARY: A beginner's guide to kayaking, with tips on choosing equipment and performing basic maneuvers and a brief history of the sport.
    ISBN 1-57572-943-1 (lib. bdg.)
    1. Kayaking Juvenile literature. [1. Kayaks and kayaking.] 1.
Title. II. Series.
GV783 .R47 1999
797.1'224--dc21   99-27663
                                                              CIP

Acknowledgments

The Publishers would like to thank the following for permission to reproduce photographs:

Action-Plus, p. 14 (Steve Bardens), p. 26 (Richard Francis); B & C Alexander, p. 4; Weymouth Canoe Lifeguard Association/Don Berry, pp. 20, 22, 23; Mountain Camera/John Cleare, pp. 18-19; Perception Kayaks, p. 7; Robert Harrison, p. 29; Tony Tickle, pp. 5, 6, 8-9, 10-13, 15-17, 21, 24, 27, 28.

Cover photograph reproduced with permission of Frank Spooner/Gamma.

Every effort has been made to contact copyright holders of any material reproduced in this book. Any omissions will be rectified in subsequent printings if notice is given to the Publisher.

Some words in this book are in bold, **like this**. You can find out what they mean by looking in the glossary.

CONTENTS

INTRODUCTION

Ancient history

Thousands of years ago, someone somewhere sat on a floating log or tree trunk and, using their hands as paddles, drifted **downstream**. Maybe a piece of wood was used as a paddle. A solid log is heavy, so the log may have been hollowed out to make it lighter. Thus the **canoe** was invented.

Further developments

In different parts of the world, early humans used whatever materials were available to build boats. Native Americans made river canoes by wrapping the bark from birch trees onto a wooden frame. The Inuit people made sealskin kayaks and sewed themselves into the **cockpit** to prevent freezing water from swamping the boat.

Today, most kayaks are made from fiberglass or plastic. Kevlar, a type of very strong lightweight fiberglass, is often used for competition designs. Plastic boats are made using **polyethylene**, a tough material that can be molded to shape.

The Inuit used their kayaks for hunting.

Canoes and kayaks

There are two main types of canoe. The open canoe, first used by Native Americans, is a sturdy craft that can carry two or three people and their possessions. The canoeist uses a single-bladed paddle and kneels on the floor of the boat. The canoe has no top surface or **deck**.

The kayak was developed from the Inuit craft and is usually for one person. The kayaker sits in the boat and uses a double-bladed paddle. A **spraydeck** covers the cockpit to prevent water from splashing into the boat—but today's **paddlers** don't sew themselves in!

This book is going to look at the single-person, decked canoe—the kayak.

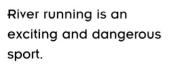

River running is an exciting and dangerous sport.

THE BOAT FOR YOU

Touring kayaks

Many experienced paddlers own several kayaks. A good kayak for beginners is the plastic touring kayak. It should have a large **cockpit** to make getting in and out easier. Kayak stores should be willing to let you try out a kayak before you buy it. Clubs will often lend a boat to new members until they have bought their own.

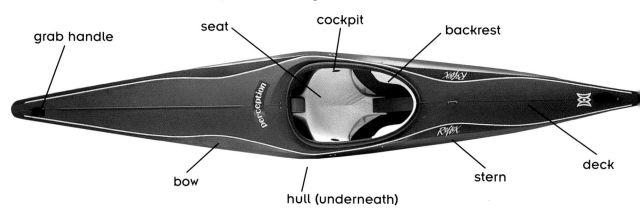

grab handle · seat · cockpit · backrest · deck · stern · hull (underneath) · bow

Essential parts

Every kayak should have something to keep it from sinking. This can be a block of plastic foam secured to the inside, or buoyancy bags filled with air and kept behind the seat. Kayaks must be fitted with a footrest and a **grab handle,** or toggle, at both ends of the boat. A fitted backrest helps. Some boats have an adjustable seat that makes it easier to achieve a snug fit.

The power that a paddler uses to propel the boat needs to be anchored. Experienced paddlers have a close footrest, backrest, and thigh grips. All of these make sure that the power of the paddle stroke goes where it should—into the water.

Kayaks can be carried by the grab handles.

KAYAK FACT

🛶 A kayak's speed depends upon its size. Longer boats are faster, and shorter ones are slower.

TOP TIP

🛶 Never try to lift a boat that is full of water. It will be too heavy. Turn it on its side to drain the water out first.

Types of boats

Boats come in all shapes and sizes. They range from touring kayaks that are suitable for beginners to high-specification expedition boats for **white-water** paddling on the world's roughest rivers. There are **slalom** kayaks, as shown on page 6, which are designed for fast turns and weigh less than five pounds. Modern kayaks need very little maintenance, and plastic boats are strong and difficult to damage.

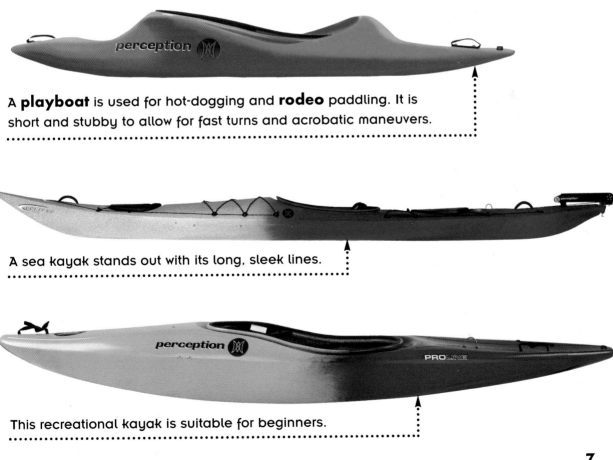

A **playboat** is used for hot-dogging and **rodeo** paddling. It is short and stubby to allow for fast turns and acrobatic maneuvers.

A sea kayak stands out with its long, sleek lines.

This recreational kayak is suitable for beginners.

WHAT ELSE DO YOU NEED?

Warmth and safety

Even on a hot summer day, rivers and lakes may be cold, so paddlers need to ensure that they are well prepared for the difference between air and water temperature. One hundred years ago, a paddler would have worn a straw hat, tweed jacket, and pants. Things have changed for today's kayakers, who have a whole wardrobe of special clothing to keep them safe and warm.

Helmet

Helmets are a must in shallow waters, fast-flowing rivers, or in the ocean. Check that your helmet fits well and has a firm chin strap. It should fit snugly so that there is no movement when you shake your head, but it should not be too tight over your forehead. Always fasten the strap.

Cagoule

A waterproof **cagoule** (cag) is an essential piece of equipment. It has an elastic neck and cuffs to keep the water out and enough room to allow you to move freely.

Personal flotation device (PFD)

A **PFD** is essential. You should never go kayaking without one. You wear your PFD like a vest. It is not a life jacket—it's filled with foam, not air. It should fit snugly with a cord or strap around your waist.

Wet suit

A wet suit is recommended, even in summer, although you can wear old sweatpants and a sweatshirt instead. A full-body wet suit is called a **steamer**. A kayaker's wet suit with no arms is a **long john**.

Footwear

Sports sandals or wet suit boots are best for your feet. Avoid thick-soled tennis shoes or shoes with long laces that could get tangled on the footrest.

Spraydeck

The **spraydeck** is worn around your waist like a skirt and fits over the rim of the **cockpit** to keep water out. As a beginner, you can start off without one, but a spraydeck makes kayaking much more comfortable.

Paddles

Paddles can be made from wood, metal, or plastic and are usually **feathered**, meaning that the blades are positioned at different angles. This allows for more natural wrist and shoulder movement. There are different paddles for different types of kayaking. Test the right paddle size for you by stretching your fingers over the top blade. Most paddles are between 75 and 83 inches (190 and 210 centimeters) long.

SAFETY TIP

In the ocean, even in summer, a swimmer's survival time without a wet suit and PFD is less than three hours. The body loses heat very quickly when it is immersed in cold water.

FIT FOR PADDLING?

Kayakers use their whole body when they make a paddle stroke. Their arms and shoulders make the stroke and their torso twists. Their legs grip the sides of the boat and their feet push against the footrest. Flexibility is often more important than strength.

Exercises

To prepare yourself for paddling, make sure you begin with a **warm-up** to stretch your muscles. This will prepare them for the work they are about to do. Jog in place for 10 minutes. Then try each of these exercises and repeat each five times.

Shoulder stretch

Begin by making large, circular movements with your arms. Keep your fingers pointed and stretch out as far as you can.

Leg stretch

Stand with your feet shoulder-width apart and slowly reach down to the ground in front of you. Continue standing and cross one leg in front of the other. Walk your fingers down the leg as far as you can. You may have to stop at the knees, or you may be able to "walk" off your toes and onto the ground. Just go as far as you feel comfortable.

Back stretch

Sit in the boat and hold the paddle in front of you. Lean back and try to make the paddle **loom** touch the rear **deck** of the boat. Now lean forward and touch the front deck.

Back and stomach stretch

While you are still in the boat, reach forward and try to make the left-hand paddle blade touch the right-hand side of the boat as far forward as you can.

SAFETY FIRST

Exercises should be done slowly to avoid pulling or tearing muscles.

Diet

Kayaking is a high-energy sport that requires a good fitness level. This means that you have to eat properly and have a balanced diet.

Sweet and fatty food is not a good basis for training. So if you want to take kayaking seriously, you should avoid chocolate and fried food. Eat healthy proteins such as fish and cheese. Fruit, vegetables, and healthy carbohydrates such as bread and baked potatoes are also good for you. Bananas offer a good mix of carbohydrates, natural sugars, and vitamins. Your body digests bananas slowly, so they are the perfect snack for a day on the water.

GETTING STARTED

At the swimming pool

The best place to learn kayaking is in a swimming pool. You need no special equipment in the pool, just a swimsuit. The water is warm, clear, and clean. If you're nervous, you can have an instructor stand by you.

Many pools have a set of kayaks and in the winter, most clubs run pool sessions for beginners and experienced paddlers. It is a good place to meet other paddlers from the local kayak club. Good clubs can offer instruction, links to national organizations such as the American Canoe Association, and a group of people ready to go kayaking with you.

In a pool, you can begin the basic strokes. You could also try these without a paddle, by using your hands.

KAYAK POLO

- Kayak polo is played in swimming pools. It is like water polo, except players use boats. Competitors wear helmets with face guards to protect them from the swinging paddles.

SAFETY FIRST

- Boats are heavy and have no brakes. Swimmers should not play in the water near **canoes** or kayaks, either in a pool or in the ocean.

········ How to get into your boat

When you take your kayak out, the first thing you need to learn is how to get into it! First, sit on the river bank next to the boat. Slide one leg into the **cockpit**, then move over until you're sitting on the rear **deck**. Slowly slide down onto the seat.

Paddling forward

To move forward, look at the front deck and imagine that you can see your feet. Hold the paddle blade away from your chest. Imagine that it's covered in bad-smelling sludge and hold it away from your nose. Place the paddle blade in the water along your toes. You need to stretch forward and twist your body. Pull the water past you. Try it on the other side.

Changing direction

To turn, place the paddle along your toes and keep your arm straight. Work the blade away from the boat through a complete arc, so it ends up behind you. The trunk of your body will twist and your foot nearest the paddle blade should be pressed hard on the footrest.

How to get out

To get out, place your hands on the deck behind you and ease your weight onto the rear deck. Slide one leg out onto the river, then slide the rest of your body out. If your paddle is strong enough, use it to keep the boat stable by resting it across the rear deck and the bank.

Peaceful places

Placid means peaceful, and placid-water kayaking takes place on canals, lakes, and slow-moving rivers. Most beginners start on placid water because it is a good place for building basic skills. In deep water, helmets are not necessary and many paddlers do not use the **spraydeck**.

Most beginners start on placid water.

Straying in a straight line

A ship moves forward because its engines push it through the water using screws at the rear. A rudder keeps a ship moving in a straight line. In a kayak, the "engine," or source of power, is you in the middle and there is no rudder. For most beginners, the result is a boat that refuses to go in a straight line! It takes time to learn the strokes. But after a couple of sessions, most people start to pick up the basics and begin to get their boat under control.

This low brace is keeping the paddler upright even though his whole weight is on the blade.

SAFETY FIRST

Never **canoe** or kayak alone. Experienced paddlers have a simple rule: "Less than three there should never be."

Staying in balance

You can get a surprising amount of support from a paddle blade. A **brace** is when the blade is laid flat on the water. It is a **support stroke** that works in a similar way to a mountain biker putting his foot down to the ground. It stabilizes the kayak as it turns.

Moving Water

Be prepared!

Moving water can indicate a fast-flowing river or ocean. In both settings, the water can sneak up on an unwary paddler. So before kayaking in moving water, make sure that you are well prepared. To survive the worst of white-water conditions, paddlers have to learn a new set of skills. The effort is worth it so that you can enjoy overcoming the elements and pitting your skills against the power of a raging river.

When entering the flow of water, raise the upstream edge of the boat with your knee and **brace** the boat with your paddle by holding it flat on the water. This is called a **break in**.

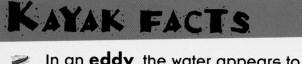

Kayak Facts

- In an **eddy**, the water appears to move uphill. In fact, it is recirculating back into the main flow. The boundary between the eddy and the flow—the eddy line—is an area of disturbed water as the fast-flowing river reacts against the quieter water of the eddy. Beware of mini-whirlpools and upflows, which paddlers call **boils**, in these areas.

A **break out** is when you leave the river flow and enter the quieter water nearer the bank called the eddy. But you still need to lean into the turn, like a biker leaning into a bend.

Special skills

If water flows onto the flat upper surface of your boat, its weight will unbalance the kayak and cause you to **capsize**. So you must "edge" **downstream** by tilting the boat slightly to keep the **upstream** edge above the water line.

Experienced paddlers will inspect a rapid to find out what hazards may lie ahead. If a section looks too dangerous, they will **portage**, or carry their boats around it. If they run the rapid, they might have **bank support**, which means that someone stands by with rescue equipment.

SAFETY FIRST

🛶 Even a slow-moving river is dangerous. You should never paddle on moving water without experienced leaders beside you to coach and assist.

River running can be an easy-going day trip down a slow meandering river or a heart-stopping, adrenaline-filled expedition requiring a support crew and exceptional kayaking skills. Either way, a kayaker needs to look out for hazards.

Stoppers

When water drops over a ledge, it forms a **stopper**. It is called a stopper because a boat running into one will stop dead in the water. Water is forced to the bottom of the river and flows **downstream** along the river bed. On the surface, water flows into the stopper. This **upstream** flow can trap kayakers and is one of the most dangerous features on any river.

Strainers

A tree in the river with water flowing through its branches is called a **strainer**. Anything that floats into the branches will be held in place by the force of the water. Avoid trees—even on slow-moving rivers.

Rocks and obstructions

Underwater rocks can **capsize** a boat, and surface rocks can trap a paddler in the same way a strainer does.

Surface water flows upstream into a stopper.

KAYAK FACTS

- In 1976, a British team led by Dr. Mike Jones paddled the Dudh Khosi, the river that flows down from Mount Everest, from a height of 17,500 feet (5300 meters). Sadly, Dr. Jones was killed trying to rescue another paddler on a later expedition.

River Grading

🛶 Rivers are graded from 1–6:

Grade 1	Not difficult. An obvious route with no obstructions.
Grade 2	Moderate. Some rapids and obstructions, but the way down is still obvious.
Grade 3	Difficult. Larger waves and rapids, obstructions, and falls. Route still recognizable.
Grade 4	Very difficult. Similar to grade 3 but the difficulties are more serious and the route is less obvious.
Grade 5	Extremely difficult. Will require a bank inspection and exceptional paddling skills.
Grade 6	Cannot be paddled without serious risk to life. Multiple obstructions and hazards, complicated route, or no clear route.

🛶 Most rivers have different grades for different sections. For example, the Zambesi in Zimbabwe is graded from 4 to 6.

This exploration boat enters a part of the Trisuli River in Nepal known as Double Rock Rapid.

Safety First

🛶 Don't rely on the river grade. Even a Grade 1 river can become dangerous in flood conditions. It is important to get information about the river from local sources.

ROCK AND ROLL

One of the most impressive tricks a kayaker can perform is the **Eskimo roll**. Experts can roll so fast that bystanders don't realize that they have **capsized** at all. There are even hand rolls in which the kayaker does not use a paddle.

In freezing water

Some kayakers perform Eskimo rolls as a stunt, but to the Inuit it was an important form of self-rescue. If an Inuit capsized, he had to escape the freezing water before it was too late. A hunting partner would put his boat along the capsized boat. The capsized Inuit would pull himself upright using the bow of his friend's boat.

This capsized kayaker performs an Eskimo rescue by using his friend's boat to pull himself upright.

Capsize drill

The best place to learn to roll is in a swimming pool where the water is clear. A diving mask will help you see what is happening under water. Before practicing the Eskimo roll, make sure you have mastered the capsize drill in which you get out of the boat while it is capsized. This is an essential skill. It means that you can leave the boat under control and without panicking. The trick is to wait until the boat is completely upside down, then push it away from you as if it were a pair of pants.

Hip flick

If you capsize, you have to use your legs and hips to swivel your boat back upright. An important part of the maneuver is the hip flick. Once you have mastered this skill, you can go on to learn the Eskimo roll. In this maneuver, the capsized paddler uses an underwater sweep to pull his or her body to the surface and the hip flick to bring the boat upright.

1. Set up with the paddle along the boat.

2. Sweep out and over your head.

3. As the boat rotates, flick your hips to keep the movement going.

SAFETY FIRST

Never practice rolling alone and always make sure that the **grab handle** on your **spraydeck** is easily available.

RESCUE

It may never happen but . . .

Kayaking is a safe activity, but sometimes things can go wrong. A hidden rock or tree branch, a wobbly beginner, or a misjudgment are all possible problems. When accidents happen, kayakers have to be ready for them.

On some beaches and at kayaking events, you may see kayak lifeguards who have been trained to use their kayaking skills to rescue people. The lifeguards on this lake are forming a raft to rescue a paddler in the water.

Throw line

Experienced paddlers will carry a full rescue kit, but anyone kayaking on a river should at least have a **throw line** and know how to use it.

Practice throwing a line. It's not as easy as it looks! If you're the person in the water requiring help, you must hold the rope to your chest and float on your back. The rescuer should "play" you like a fish by pulling you slowly towards the bank. If there is too much tension on the rope, it will be difficult to hold on.

In an x-rescue, the rescuer empties the victim's boat.

X-rescue

In deep water in the ocean or on a lake where there is no bank nearby, the **x-rescue** can be important. It involves getting the victim back into his or her boat. As the rescuer, you pull the victim's flooded boat across your **deck** and tilt it to empty out the water. This is harder than it sounds because a flooded boat is heavy.

The victim waits in the water with the paddles and holds on to the **grab handle** at the front of your boat. When the victim's boat is empty, he or she can get back into the kayak while you hold it steady.

SAFETY FIRST

- Never tie yourself or anyone else to a rope while kayaking, even in a rescue. The risk of getting tangled up is too high.

RESCUE KIT

- Throw line: 30 feet (9 meters) of strong rope that floats on water

- Loops and **carabiners**: used to set up a pulley to extract a trapped boat

- Survival bag: keeps the victim warm until help arrives

- First aid kit: container should be waterproof

Sea kayaks are much closer to the original Inuit craft than plastic river boats. Sea paddlers have rounded Cape Horn, paddled arount the British Isles, crossed the Tasmanian Sea, and traversed the Great Lakes. The boats are long, sleek, and fast, with **deck** hatches for storing food and equipment.

Sea kayaks are silent and can go close to shore where other boats would run aground. As a result, sea paddlers can get close to wildlife like seals and birds.

Avoiding difficulties

Sea paddlers must be able to navigate and understand the weather. A wrong decision could lead to disaster. In difficult ocean conditions, the paddler must use the paddle as a rudder. This **stern rudder** keeps the sea boat from broadsiding or **broaching**.

Surf's up

Surf kayakers use special kayaks or **surf skis** in the same way that surfers use their boards to ride the energy of the waves onto the beach. A surf kayak can travel at speeds of 18 miles (29 kilometers) per hour or more.

The trick is to wait for a wave to form and then paddle hard into shore to match its speed. After the wave picks up your kayak, use your paddle as a stern rudder to keep the boat on line, **peeling off** the wave as it breaks.

KAYAK FACTS

> ✏ The water in a surf wave is going nowhere. It appears to rush toward the beach, but there is only movement at the very edge. Waves are a result of the wind pushing against the water and creating an up and down movement called a swell. The waves crashing onto Bondi beach in Australia were born far out in the ocean, sometimes thousands of miles away.

SAFETY FIRST

> ✏ Don't try paddle surfing if you're a beginner, because it requires a lot of skill. An out-of-control kayaker can be a danger not only to the kayaker but to other people in the water. Sea paddlers also need to be aware of tides and currents. Never take a boat onto the ocean without checking these conditions. Contact the coast guard for information.

Paddle surfing can be a lot of fun, but make sure you know about the ocean conditions first.

COMPETITIONS

There are a number of competitive kayaking events ranging from Olympic **slalom** to marathon racing. There are also various extreme forms of kayaking, including waterfall running! As the number of kayakers increases, so does the number of competitions. There are opportunities for every level of kayaker, from beginners to Olympic contenders.

Slalom

Slalom is an Olympic event, and competitions take place on river rapids. The paddlers try to run the course as fast as they can. Pairs of light poles hanging over the water act as gates. A course can have up to 25 gates.

Paddlers have to go **downstream** through green gates and **upstream** through red ones. Slalom boats are usually made from fiberglass for lightness and strength. They are designed for speed and maneuverability.

Anyone can compete in slalom. Events range from beginners' events, which any paddler can enter, to international competitions.

Paddlers must try to go through the slalom gate without touching the poles.

Sprint

The sprint involves kayak racing over placid water and is the other Olympic kayaking event. Distances are raced from 650 feet (200 meters) to about 6.2 miles (10,000 meters). Boats can have a crew of four.

White-water racing

This involves kayakers paddling down a Grade 3 or 4 river as fast as they can. The course is usually about 30 minutes long. The racing boats' wing design helps with speed and stability.

Rodeo

Since the development of short plastic **playboats**, a new kayak sport has taken off. It's called **rodeo**, and the idea is to perform all kinds of acrobatics with the boat. Paddlers use the power of a river wave to stand the boat on end, throw it in the air, or spin around in a cartwheel. Points are awarded for each move. It's amazing what some paddlers can make their boats do!

A member of the Japanese team performing a **pop out** at a rodeo competition in Australia.

Olympics

French slalomist Myriam Jerusalmi took the bronze medal in the 1996 Atlanta Olympics. The women's gold medal went to Czech Stepanka Hilgertova, and German Oliver Fix took the men's gold medal.

1998 Slalom World Cup

World champion Paul Ratcliffe of the United Kingdom scraped ahead of American Scott Shipley in the 1998 **Slalom** World Cup. Stepanka Hilgertova took the women's number one position.

Paul Ratcliffe was the 1998 world champion in the slalom event.

Jamie Simon

One of the world's foremost **rodeo** stars is Jamie Simon of the United States. She won the World Kayak Federation's championship in 1995 and placed third in 1997. In 1998, her run over a 44-foot (13.5-meter) waterfall in California was broadcast on national television. Along with Dana Chladek, who competes in slalom events, she is leading the way for women paddlers everywhere.

Dana Chladek from the United States won the women's silver medal in the 1996 Atlanta Olympics.

KAYAK FACTS

🜂 In World War II, the Royal Marines in Great Britain used canvas kayaks to carry out a raid on the port of Bordeaux in occupied France. The kayaks were folded so that they could be passed through the hatch of a submarine. The raid was led by Major "Blondie" Hasler.

GLOSSARY

bank support paddlers who stand by with rescue gear while another paddler "runs" the rapid

boil swirl of water caused by the friction between the river flow and an eddy. A boil can be very violent.

brace support stroke

break in to enter the flow of a river

break out to leave the flow or enter an eddy

broach when a kayak is forced sideways onto a wave (often leads to a capsize)

cagoule waterproof top with elastic neck and cuffs, designed to keep kayakers dry

canoe small boat paddled by someone facing in the direction of travel

capsize when a boat turns upside down

carabiner oval of strong metal with an opening gate. It can be clipped onto fences, ropes, boats, or your PFD.

cockpit where the paddler sits in a kayak

deck upper surface of a boat

downstream (or down river) direction the water is flowing

eddy quiet stretch of water near a river bank or an obstruction such as a rock

Eskimo roll type of self-rescue maneuver

feathered describes paddle blades that are not parallel to each other

grab handle loop or toggle at the front and back of a kayak

long john lightweight wet suit with no arms

loom part of the paddle between the blades that you hold onto

neoprene elastic material that acts as an insulator even when it is wet

outrigger pole or hull attached to a boat to provide additional stability

peeling off turning sideways and back out to the ocean to avoid being swept onto the shore by the breaking wave

PFD (Personal Flotation Device) jacket padded with foam used to keep a swimmer afloat

playboat short plastic boat designed for unusual maneuvers

polyethylene strong durable plastic that can be molded into different shapes

pop out rodeo maneuver in which the paddler forces the boat to exit vertically from the water

portage to walk around a rapid or obstruction

rodeo (also called freestyle paddling) kayak competition in which paddlers have to perform acrobatics in their boats

slalom kayak race using gates

spraydeck cover for the cockpit worn by the kayaker as a skirt and attached to the cockpit rim

steamer full-body wet suit normally worn by scuba divers. It restricts movement and is rarely used by kayakers.

stern rudder steering stroke used by surfers

stopper dangerous recirculating river wave. It is also called a hole.

strainer tree in the river with water running through its branches

support stroke either a brace to provide stability during a turn or a quick slap against the water surface used to regain balance

surf ski combination of a surf board and kayak where the paddler sits on the board

throw line kayaker's rescue rope, made from brightly colored, floating material

upstream direction the water is coming from

warm-up exercises done to prepare the body for kayaking

white water general term for rivers of Grade 2 and above. Rapids cause aeration of the water (air bubbles) that makes it look white. Rapids are sometimes called wild water.

x-rescue deep-water assisted rescue technique

USEFUL ADDRESSES

Kayaking has become so popular that you can find local clubs almost anywhere. Your local boat shop is a good place to find out about clubs and competitions. You can also look in kayaking magazines and on the Internet. Here are addresses for some of the national and international kayaking organizations. They run most of the larger competitions and are good sources of information on kayaking events.

American Canoe Association (ACA)
7432 Alban Station Blvd., Suite B-232
Springfield, VA 22150
703-451-0141

American Whitewater Affiliation
P.O. Box 636
16 Bull Run Road
Margaret, NY 12455

U.S. Canoe and Kayak Team
P.O. Box 789
Lake Placid, NY 12946

World Kayak Federation
P.O. Box 138
Glenn Echo, MD 20812

International Canoe Federation
1143.Budapest
Dózsa György 't 1-3
Hungary

MORE BOOKS TO READ

Bach, Julie. *Kayaking*. Mankato, Minn.: Smart Apple Media, 2000.

Evans, Jeremy. *Whitewater Kayaking*. Parsippany, N.J.: Silver Burdett Press, 1992.

Fox, Alan. *Kayaking*. Minneapolis: The Lerner Publishing Group, 1993.

Lund, Bill. *Kayaking*. Danbury, Conn.: Children's Press, 1996.

INDEX